50 Delicious Premium Noodle Recipes

By: Kelly Johnson

Table of Contents

- Truffle Alfredo Fettuccine
- Lobster Mac and Cheese
- Pad Thai with Shrimp
- Szechuan Spicy Noodles
- Korean Japchae (Sweet Potato Noodles)
- Pesto Pasta with Grilled Chicken
- Seafood Linguine in White Wine Sauce
- Fettuccine Carbonara
- Wild Mushroom Risotto with Fettuccine
- Zucchini Noodles with Avocado Sauce
- Butternut Squash Ravioli with Sage Brown Butter
- Baked Ziti with Ricotta and Mozzarella
- Miso Ramen with Soft-Boiled Eggs
- Thai Drunken Noodles (Pad Kee Mao)
- Duck Confit Pasta
- Spaghetti Aglio e Olio with Shrimp
- Seafood Udon Noodle Soup
- Linguine with Clam Sauce
- Soba Noodle Salad with Sesame Dressing
- Lemon Garlic Shrimp Pasta
- Pappardelle with Braised Short Ribs
- Spinach and Ricotta Stuffed Shells
- Beef Stroganoff with Egg Noodles
- Cacio e Pepe
- Fried Udon Noodles with Vegetables
- Chili Garlic Noodles
- Mushroom and Pea Risotto
- Vegan Pad See Ew
- Creamy Garlic Parmesan Pasta
- Bolognese Tagliatelle
- Cold Soba Noodles with Dipping Sauce
- Pork and Cabbage Dumplings with Noodles
- Noodle Soup with Tofu and Vegetables
- Spinach and Feta Pasta Bake
- Coconut Curry Noodles

- Prawn and Mango Noodle Salad
- Fettuccine Primavera
- Sweet and Spicy Noodles with Peanut Sauce
- Noodles with Miso Butter and Scallions
- Wild Mushroom and Truffle Oil Pasta
- Chicken Lo Mein
- Sesame Noodles with Grilled Chicken
- Baked Macaroni and Cheese with Bacon
- Lemon Basil Pasta with Grilled Shrimp
- Spaghetti with Roasted Garlic and Broccoli
- Cheesy Italian Pasta Bake
- Vegetable Lo Mein
- Alfredo Zoodles (Zucchini Noodles)
- Pasta with Roasted Red Pepper Sauce
- Black Bean Noodles with Avocado and Lime

Truffle Alfredo Fettuccine

Ingredients:

- 12 oz fettuccine pasta
- 1 cup heavy cream
- 1/2 cup grated Parmesan cheese
- 1/4 cup unsalted butter
- 1-2 tbsp truffle oil (to taste)
- Salt and pepper to taste
- Fresh parsley for garnish

Instructions:

1. Cook the fettuccine according to package instructions; drain and set aside.
2. In a large skillet, melt the butter over medium heat.
3. Add the heavy cream and bring to a gentle simmer.
4. Stir in the Parmesan cheese until melted and smooth.
5. Add the cooked fettuccine to the skillet, tossing to coat.
6. Drizzle with truffle oil, and season with salt and pepper.
7. Garnish with fresh parsley before serving.

Lobster Mac and Cheese

Ingredients:

- 8 oz elbow macaroni
- 2 cups shredded cheddar cheese
- 1 cup milk
- 1/2 cup heavy cream
- 1/4 cup unsalted butter
- 1/4 cup all-purpose flour
- 1 cup cooked lobster meat, chopped
- Salt and pepper to taste
- Breadcrumbs for topping

Instructions:

1. Preheat the oven to 350°F (175°C).
2. Cook the macaroni according to package instructions; drain and set aside.
3. In a saucepan, melt the butter over medium heat, then whisk in the flour to form a roux.
4. Gradually whisk in the milk and heavy cream until smooth and thickened.
5. Stir in the cheddar cheese until melted.
6. Combine the cheese sauce with the macaroni and lobster meat; season with salt and pepper.
7. Transfer to a baking dish, top with breadcrumbs, and bake for 20-25 minutes until golden.

Pad Thai with Shrimp

Ingredients:

- 8 oz rice noodles
- 1 lb shrimp, peeled and deveined
- 2 eggs, lightly beaten
- 2 tbsp fish sauce
- 2 tbsp tamarind paste
- 1 tbsp sugar
- 2 cloves garlic, minced
- 1 cup bean sprouts
- 1/4 cup chopped green onions
- Lime wedges and crushed peanuts for serving

Instructions:

1. Cook the rice noodles according to package instructions; drain and set aside.
2. In a large skillet, sauté garlic until fragrant, then add shrimp and cook until pink.
3. Push shrimp to one side, pour beaten eggs into the skillet, and scramble.
4. Stir in the cooked noodles, fish sauce, tamarind paste, and sugar.
5. Add bean sprouts and green onions, tossing to combine.
6. Serve with lime wedges and crushed peanuts.

Szechuan Spicy Noodles

Ingredients:

- 8 oz noodles (egg or rice)
- 2 tbsp Szechuan peppercorns
- 2 tbsp soy sauce
- 1 tbsp chili oil
- 1 tbsp sesame oil
- 2 cloves garlic, minced
- 1 cup mixed vegetables (carrots, bell peppers, broccoli)
- Chopped scallions for garnish

Instructions:

1. Cook the noodles according to package instructions; drain and set aside.
2. In a pan, heat the Szechuan peppercorns in sesame oil until fragrant, then add garlic and vegetables.
3. Stir-fry until vegetables are tender.
4. Add the cooked noodles, soy sauce, and chili oil, tossing to coat.
5. Garnish with chopped scallions before serving.

Korean Japchae (Sweet Potato Noodles)

Ingredients:

- 8 oz sweet potato noodles
- 1 cup spinach
- 1/2 cup sliced mushrooms
- 1/2 cup sliced bell peppers
- 1/2 cup carrots, julienned
- 2 tbsp soy sauce
- 1 tbsp sesame oil
- 1 tbsp sugar
- 2 cloves garlic, minced

Instructions:

1. Cook sweet potato noodles according to package instructions; drain and set aside.
2. In a pan, heat sesame oil and sauté garlic, mushrooms, and vegetables until tender.
3. Add the spinach and cook until wilted.
4. Stir in the noodles, soy sauce, and sugar, mixing well.
5. Serve hot or at room temperature.

Pesto Pasta with Grilled Chicken

Ingredients:

- 12 oz pasta (penne or fusilli)
- 1 cup pesto sauce
- 1 lb grilled chicken, sliced
- 1/4 cup grated Parmesan cheese
- Cherry tomatoes for garnish

Instructions:

1. Cook the pasta according to package instructions; drain and set aside.
2. In a large bowl, combine the cooked pasta with pesto sauce.
3. Top with grilled chicken and toss gently to combine.
4. Garnish with grated Parmesan and cherry tomatoes before serving.

Seafood Linguine in White Wine Sauce

Ingredients:

- 8 oz linguine
- 1 cup mixed seafood (shrimp, mussels, clams)
- 1/2 cup white wine
- 2 cloves garlic, minced
- 1/4 cup chopped parsley
- 1/4 cup olive oil
- Salt and pepper to taste

Instructions:

1. Cook linguine according to package instructions; drain and set aside.
2. In a large skillet, heat olive oil and sauté garlic until fragrant.
3. Add mixed seafood and cook until opaque, then pour in white wine.
4. Simmer until slightly reduced, then stir in cooked linguine and parsley.
5. Season with salt and pepper before serving.

Fettuccine Carbonara

Ingredients:

- 12 oz fettuccine
- 4 oz pancetta or bacon, diced
- 2 large eggs
- 1/2 cup grated Parmesan cheese
- 2 cloves garlic, minced
- Salt and pepper to taste
- Fresh parsley for garnish

Instructions:

1. Cook fettuccine according to package instructions; drain and set aside.
2. In a skillet, cook pancetta or bacon until crispy; add garlic and sauté for 1 minute.
3. In a bowl, whisk together eggs and Parmesan cheese.
4. Combine the hot fettuccine with the pancetta mixture, then quickly stir in the egg mixture until creamy.
5. Season with salt and pepper, and garnish with fresh parsley before serving.

Wild Mushroom Risotto with Fettuccine

Ingredients:

- 8 oz fettuccine
- 1 cup Arborio rice
- 4 cups vegetable or chicken broth
- 1 cup mixed wild mushrooms, sliced
- 1 small onion, finely chopped
- 2 cloves garlic, minced
- 1/2 cup white wine
- 1/2 cup grated Parmesan cheese
- 2 tbsp olive oil
- Salt and pepper to taste
- Fresh parsley for garnish

Instructions:

1. In a pot, bring the broth to a simmer and keep warm.
2. In a large skillet, heat olive oil over medium heat. Sauté onion and garlic until translucent.
3. Add the mushrooms and cook until softened.
4. Stir in Arborio rice, cooking for about 2 minutes.
5. Pour in white wine and stir until absorbed.
6. Gradually add warm broth, one ladle at a time, stirring constantly until absorbed before adding more.
7. Cook until the rice is creamy and al dente (about 20 minutes).
8. Cook fettuccine according to package instructions; drain.
9. Mix cooked fettuccine with the risotto. Stir in Parmesan, season with salt and pepper, and garnish with parsley before serving.

Zucchini Noodles with Avocado Sauce

Ingredients:

- 4 medium zucchinis, spiralized into noodles
- 1 ripe avocado
- 2 tbsp lemon juice
- 1 clove garlic
- 1/4 cup fresh basil leaves
- Salt and pepper to taste
- Cherry tomatoes for garnish

Instructions:

1. In a food processor, combine avocado, lemon juice, garlic, basil, salt, and pepper. Blend until smooth.
2. In a large skillet, lightly sauté zucchini noodles for about 2-3 minutes until slightly softened.
3. Toss the noodles with the avocado sauce until well coated.
4. Serve garnished with cherry tomatoes.

Butternut Squash Ravioli with Sage Brown Butter

Ingredients:

- 12 oz butternut squash ravioli
- 4 tbsp unsalted butter
- 6 fresh sage leaves
- 1/4 cup grated Parmesan cheese
- Salt and pepper to taste

Instructions:

1. Cook ravioli according to package instructions; drain.
2. In a skillet, melt butter over medium heat. Add sage leaves and cook until butter is golden and fragrant.
3. Add the cooked ravioli to the skillet, tossing gently to coat in the brown butter.
4. Season with salt and pepper and serve topped with grated Parmesan.

Baked Ziti with Ricotta and Mozzarella

Ingredients:

- 12 oz ziti pasta
- 2 cups marinara sauce
- 1 cup ricotta cheese
- 2 cups shredded mozzarella cheese
- 1/2 cup grated Parmesan cheese
- 1 egg
- 1 tsp Italian seasoning
- Salt and pepper to taste

Instructions:

1. Preheat the oven to 350°F (175°C).
2. Cook ziti according to package instructions; drain and set aside.
3. In a bowl, mix ricotta, egg, Italian seasoning, salt, and pepper.
4. Combine cooked ziti with marinara sauce and half of the mozzarella.
5. In a baking dish, layer half of the ziti mixture, then the ricotta mixture, and top with the remaining ziti.
6. Sprinkle with the remaining mozzarella and Parmesan cheese.
7. Bake for 25-30 minutes until bubbly and golden.

Miso Ramen with Soft-Boiled Eggs

Ingredients:

- 4 oz ramen noodles
- 4 cups chicken or vegetable broth
- 2 tbsp miso paste
- 2 soft-boiled eggs
- 1 cup spinach
- 1/2 cup sliced green onions
- 1/2 cup sliced mushrooms
- Soy sauce to taste

Instructions:

1. Cook ramen noodles according to package instructions; drain.
2. In a pot, heat the broth and stir in miso paste until dissolved.
3. Add mushrooms and spinach, cooking until tender.
4. Divide the noodles into bowls and ladle broth over them.
5. Top with soft-boiled eggs, green onions, and soy sauce before serving.

Thai Drunken Noodles (Pad Kee Mao)

Ingredients:

- 8 oz wide rice noodles
- 1 cup mixed vegetables (bell peppers, broccoli, carrots)
- 1 lb chicken or shrimp, sliced
- 2 cloves garlic, minced
- 2 tbsp soy sauce
- 2 tbsp oyster sauce
- 1 tbsp fish sauce
- 1 tsp chili paste (adjust to taste)
- Basil leaves for garnish

Instructions:

1. Cook rice noodles according to package instructions; drain and set aside.
2. In a large skillet or wok, sauté garlic in oil until fragrant.
3. Add chicken or shrimp and cook until done.
4. Stir in mixed vegetables, cooking until tender.
5. Add cooked noodles and sauces, tossing everything together.
6. Garnish with fresh basil leaves before serving.

Duck Confit Pasta

Ingredients:

- 8 oz pasta (pappardelle or tagliatelle)
- 2 duck confit legs, shredded
- 1 cup duck fat (or olive oil)
- 1/2 cup heavy cream
- 1/4 cup grated Parmesan cheese
- Salt and pepper to taste
- Fresh thyme for garnish

Instructions:

1. Cook pasta according to package instructions; drain and reserve some pasta water.
2. In a skillet, melt duck fat over medium heat. Add shredded duck confit and sauté until crispy.
3. Stir in heavy cream and Parmesan, cooking until heated through.
4. Toss in cooked pasta, adding reserved pasta water if needed for creaminess.
5. Season with salt and pepper, and garnish with fresh thyme before serving.

Spaghetti Aglio e Olio with Shrimp

Ingredients:

- 8 oz spaghetti
- 1 lb shrimp, peeled and deveined
- 4 cloves garlic, thinly sliced
- 1/2 tsp red pepper flakes (adjust to taste)
- 1/4 cup olive oil
- Salt and pepper to taste
- Fresh parsley for garnish

Instructions:

1. Cook spaghetti according to package instructions; drain and reserve some pasta water.
2. In a large skillet, heat olive oil over medium heat. Add garlic and red pepper flakes, cooking until garlic is golden.
3. Add shrimp, cooking until pink and opaque.
4. Toss in the cooked spaghetti, adding reserved pasta water if necessary to loosen the sauce.
5. Season with salt and pepper, and garnish with fresh parsley before serving.

Seafood Udon Noodle Soup

Ingredients:

- 8 oz udon noodles
- 4 cups seafood stock
- 1 cup mixed seafood (shrimp, scallops, fish)
- 1 cup bok choy, chopped
- 2 green onions, sliced
- 2 cloves garlic, minced
- 1 tbsp ginger, minced
- 2 tbsp soy sauce
- 1 tbsp sesame oil
- Salt and pepper to taste
- Fresh cilantro for garnish

Instructions:

1. Cook udon noodles according to package instructions; drain and set aside.
2. In a pot, heat sesame oil over medium heat. Sauté garlic and ginger until fragrant.
3. Add seafood stock and bring to a simmer. Stir in soy sauce and mixed seafood.
4. Cook until seafood is just done. Add bok choy and noodles, simmering for an additional 2-3 minutes.
5. Season with salt and pepper, garnish with green onions and cilantro before serving.

Linguine with Clam Sauce

Ingredients:

- 12 oz linguine
- 2 cans (6.5 oz each) chopped clams, drained (reserve juice)
- 1/4 cup olive oil
- 4 cloves garlic, minced
- 1/2 cup white wine
- 1/2 tsp red pepper flakes (optional)
- 1/4 cup fresh parsley, chopped
- Salt and pepper to taste

Instructions:

1. Cook linguine according to package instructions; reserve some pasta water and drain.
2. In a large skillet, heat olive oil over medium heat. Add garlic and red pepper flakes, sautéing until fragrant.
3. Pour in white wine and cook for 2 minutes, then add reserved clam juice and clams.
4. Simmer for 5 minutes, then add cooked linguine and toss to combine.
5. Season with salt and pepper, garnish with parsley, and serve immediately.

Soba Noodle Salad with Sesame Dressing

Ingredients:

- 8 oz soba noodles
- 1 cup shredded carrots
- 1 cup cucumber, julienned
- 1 red bell pepper, sliced
- 1/4 cup green onions, sliced
- 1/4 cup sesame seeds

For the Dressing:

- 3 tbsp soy sauce
- 2 tbsp rice vinegar
- 1 tbsp sesame oil
- 1 tsp honey or maple syrup
- 1 tsp grated ginger

Instructions:

1. Cook soba noodles according to package instructions; drain and rinse under cold water.
2. In a bowl, whisk together dressing ingredients.
3. In a large bowl, combine noodles, carrots, cucumber, bell pepper, and green onions.
4. Pour dressing over the salad and toss to coat.
5. Sprinkle with sesame seeds before serving.

Lemon Garlic Shrimp Pasta

Ingredients:

- 8 oz spaghetti or linguine
- 1 lb shrimp, peeled and deveined
- 4 cloves garlic, minced
- 1/4 cup olive oil
- Zest and juice of 1 lemon
- 1/4 tsp red pepper flakes (optional)
- Salt and pepper to taste
- Fresh parsley for garnish

Instructions:

1. Cook pasta according to package instructions; reserve some pasta water and drain.
2. In a large skillet, heat olive oil over medium heat. Sauté garlic until fragrant, then add shrimp.
3. Cook shrimp until pink, about 3-4 minutes.
4. Add lemon zest, juice, red pepper flakes, salt, and pepper, stirring to combine.
5. Toss in the cooked pasta, adding reserved pasta water to reach desired consistency.
6. Garnish with parsley and serve.

Pappardelle with Braised Short Ribs

Ingredients:

- 1 lb pappardelle
- 2 lbs short ribs
- 1 onion, chopped
- 2 carrots, chopped
- 2 celery stalks, chopped
- 4 cloves garlic, minced
- 2 cups beef broth
- 1 cup red wine
- 1 bay leaf
- Salt and pepper to taste
- Fresh parsley for garnish

Instructions:

1. Preheat oven to 325°F (165°C).
2. In a large oven-safe pot, heat oil over medium heat. Sear short ribs on all sides; remove and set aside.
3. In the same pot, add onion, carrots, celery, and garlic, cooking until softened.
4. Add red wine, scraping the bottom of the pot, and bring to a simmer.
5. Return short ribs to the pot, add beef broth and bay leaf, and cover.
6. Braise in the oven for about 2.5-3 hours until tender.
7. Cook pappardelle according to package instructions; drain.
8. Serve short ribs over pasta, garnished with parsley.

Spinach and Ricotta Stuffed Shells

Ingredients:

- 12 oz jumbo pasta shells
- 2 cups ricotta cheese
- 1 cup spinach, cooked and chopped
- 1/2 cup grated Parmesan cheese
- 2 cups marinara sauce
- 1 cup shredded mozzarella cheese
- 1 egg
- Salt and pepper to taste

Instructions:

1. Preheat the oven to 375°F (190°C).
2. Cook shells according to package instructions; drain and set aside.
3. In a bowl, mix ricotta, spinach, egg, Parmesan, salt, and pepper.
4. Fill each shell with the ricotta mixture and place in a baking dish.
5. Pour marinara sauce over the shells and top with mozzarella.
6. Bake for 25-30 minutes until bubbly and golden.

Beef Stroganoff with Egg Noodles

Ingredients:

- 12 oz egg noodles
- 1 lb beef sirloin, sliced thin
- 1 onion, sliced
- 8 oz mushrooms, sliced
- 2 cups beef broth
- 1 cup sour cream
- 2 tbsp flour
- 2 tbsp olive oil
- Salt and pepper to taste
- Fresh parsley for garnish

Instructions:

1. Cook egg noodles according to package instructions; drain.
2. In a skillet, heat olive oil over medium heat. Sauté onions until translucent, then add mushrooms and cook until soft.
3. Push vegetables to the side, add beef, and cook until browned.
4. Sprinkle flour over the mixture, stir to combine, and cook for 1-2 minutes.
5. Gradually add beef broth, stirring until thickened.
6. Remove from heat and stir in sour cream, seasoning with salt and pepper.
7. Serve over egg noodles, garnished with parsley.

Cacio e Pepe

Ingredients:

- 12 oz spaghetti
- 1 cup grated Pecorino Romano cheese
- 1/2 cup freshly cracked black pepper
- Salt to taste

Instructions:

1. Cook spaghetti according to package instructions; reserve some pasta water and drain.
2. In a large skillet, toast cracked black pepper over medium heat for 1-2 minutes.
3. Add drained spaghetti to the skillet, tossing to coat in the pepper.
4. Gradually add reserved pasta water, stirring until the sauce thickens.
5. Remove from heat and stir in Pecorino Romano cheese until creamy.
6. Serve immediately with extra cheese and black pepper on top.

Enjoy these wonderful pasta and noodle dishes!

Fried Udon Noodles with Vegetables

Ingredients:

- 8 oz udon noodles
- 1 cup bell peppers, sliced
- 1 cup carrots, julienned
- 1 cup broccoli florets
- 1 cup snow peas
- 3 green onions, sliced
- 3 tbsp soy sauce
- 1 tbsp oyster sauce (optional)
- 2 tbsp sesame oil
- 1 tbsp vegetable oil
- 2 cloves garlic, minced
- Salt and pepper to taste

Instructions:

1. Cook udon noodles according to package instructions; drain and set aside.
2. Heat vegetable oil in a large skillet or wok over medium-high heat. Add garlic and sauté for 30 seconds.
3. Add bell peppers, carrots, broccoli, and snow peas; stir-fry for 3-4 minutes until tender.
4. Add cooked udon noodles, soy sauce, oyster sauce, and sesame oil. Toss to combine and heat through.
5. Season with salt and pepper, and garnish with green onions before serving.

Chili Garlic Noodles

Ingredients:

- 8 oz spaghetti or egg noodles
- 3 tbsp soy sauce
- 2 tbsp chili paste or sauce
- 4 cloves garlic, minced
- 2 tbsp vegetable oil
- 1/4 cup green onions, sliced
- 1 tbsp sesame oil
- Salt to taste

Instructions:

1. Cook noodles according to package instructions; drain and set aside.
2. In a large skillet, heat vegetable oil over medium heat. Sauté garlic until fragrant.
3. Add chili paste and cook for an additional minute.
4. Add cooked noodles, soy sauce, and sesame oil; toss to combine.
5. Season with salt and garnish with green onions before serving.

Mushroom and Pea Risotto

Ingredients:

- 1 cup Arborio rice
- 4 cups vegetable broth
- 1 cup mushrooms, sliced
- 1/2 cup peas (fresh or frozen)
- 1 onion, chopped
- 2 cloves garlic, minced
- 1/2 cup white wine (optional)
- 1/2 cup grated Parmesan cheese
- 2 tbsp olive oil
- Salt and pepper to taste

Instructions:

1. Heat vegetable broth in a pot and keep it warm.
2. In a large skillet, heat olive oil over medium heat. Add onion and garlic; sauté until softened.
3. Add mushrooms and cook until browned. Stir in Arborio rice and cook for 1-2 minutes until translucent.
4. Pour in white wine (if using) and cook until absorbed.
5. Gradually add warm vegetable broth, one ladle at a time, stirring frequently until absorbed.
6. Stir in peas and cook for an additional 5 minutes. Remove from heat and stir in Parmesan cheese.
7. Season with salt and pepper before serving.

Vegan Pad See Ew

Ingredients:

- 8 oz wide rice noodles
- 1 cup broccoli florets
- 1 cup bell peppers, sliced
- 1 cup carrots, julienned
- 1/4 cup soy sauce
- 2 tbsp dark soy sauce (optional)
- 2 tbsp vegetable oil
- 2 cloves garlic, minced
- 1 tbsp sugar (brown or coconut)
- 1 tsp sesame oil
- Fresh lime wedges for serving

Instructions:

1. Cook rice noodles according to package instructions; drain and set aside.
2. Heat vegetable oil in a large skillet or wok over medium-high heat. Sauté garlic until fragrant.
3. Add broccoli, bell peppers, and carrots; stir-fry for 3-4 minutes until tender.
4. Add cooked noodles, soy sauce, dark soy sauce, sugar, and sesame oil; toss to combine.
5. Cook for an additional 2-3 minutes until heated through. Serve with lime wedges.

Creamy Garlic Parmesan Pasta

Ingredients:

- 12 oz fettuccine or linguine
- 3/4 cup heavy cream
- 1 cup grated Parmesan cheese
- 4 cloves garlic, minced
- 2 tbsp butter
- 1/4 tsp nutmeg (optional)
- Salt and pepper to taste
- Fresh parsley for garnish

Instructions:

1. Cook pasta according to package instructions; reserve some pasta water and drain.
2. In a large skillet, melt butter over medium heat. Add garlic and sauté until fragrant.
3. Pour in heavy cream and simmer for 2-3 minutes. Stir in Parmesan cheese until melted and smooth.
4. Add reserved pasta water as needed for consistency. Season with nutmeg, salt, and pepper.
5. Toss in cooked pasta and combine well. Garnish with parsley before serving.

Bolognese Tagliatelle

Ingredients:

- 12 oz tagliatelle
- 1 lb ground beef or a mix of beef and pork
- 1 onion, chopped
- 2 carrots, chopped
- 2 celery stalks, chopped
- 4 cloves garlic, minced
- 1 can (14 oz) crushed tomatoes
- 1/2 cup red wine
- 1/2 cup milk
- 2 tbsp olive oil
- Salt and pepper to taste
- Fresh basil for garnish

Instructions:

1. Cook tagliatelle according to package instructions; drain and set aside.
2. In a large skillet, heat olive oil over medium heat. Add onion, carrots, and celery; sauté until softened.
3. Add garlic and ground meat, cooking until browned. Drain excess fat if needed.
4. Pour in red wine and let it simmer until reduced. Stir in crushed tomatoes and milk, simmering for 20-30 minutes.
5. Season with salt and pepper. Serve sauce over tagliatelle, garnished with fresh basil.

Cold Soba Noodles with Dipping Sauce

Ingredients:

- 8 oz soba noodles
- 1/4 cup soy sauce
- 1/4 cup mirin
- 1 tbsp rice vinegar
- 1 tbsp sesame oil
- 1 green onion, sliced
- 1 tbsp grated ginger
- Nori sheets for garnish (optional)

Instructions:

1. Cook soba noodles according to package instructions; drain and rinse under cold water.
2. In a bowl, whisk together soy sauce, mirin, rice vinegar, sesame oil, green onion, and ginger to make the dipping sauce.
3. Serve cold soba noodles with dipping sauce on the side. Garnish with nori sheets if desired.

Pork and Cabbage Dumplings with Noodles

Ingredients:

- 8 oz egg noodles
- 1 lb ground pork
- 2 cups cabbage, finely chopped
- 2 green onions, chopped
- 2 cloves garlic, minced
- 1 tbsp soy sauce
- 1 tbsp ginger, minced
- 1 tbsp sesame oil
- Salt and pepper to taste

Instructions:

1. Cook egg noodles according to package instructions; drain and set aside.
2. In a large bowl, mix ground pork, cabbage, green onions, garlic, soy sauce, ginger, sesame oil, salt, and pepper until well combined.
3. Form mixture into small dumplings (about 1 inch).
4. Steam dumplings for 10-12 minutes until cooked through.
5. Serve dumplings over cooked noodles, drizzling with additional soy sauce if desired.

Noodle Soup with Tofu and Vegetables

Ingredients:

- 8 oz rice noodles
- 1 block (14 oz) firm tofu, cubed
- 4 cups vegetable broth
- 1 cup bok choy, chopped
- 1 cup carrots, sliced
- 1 cup mushrooms, sliced
- 1 bell pepper, sliced
- 2 green onions, sliced
- 3 cloves garlic, minced
- 1 tbsp soy sauce
- 1 tbsp sesame oil
- Fresh cilantro for garnish

Instructions:

1. Cook rice noodles according to package instructions; drain and set aside.
2. In a large pot, heat sesame oil over medium heat. Add garlic and sauté until fragrant.
3. Pour in vegetable broth, add soy sauce, and bring to a simmer.
4. Add bok choy, carrots, mushrooms, and bell pepper; cook until vegetables are tender (about 5-7 minutes).
5. Add cubed tofu and cooked noodles; gently stir to heat through.
6. Serve hot, garnished with green onions and fresh cilantro.

Spinach and Feta Pasta Bake

Ingredients:

- 12 oz penne or fusilli pasta
- 2 cups fresh spinach
- 1 cup crumbled feta cheese
- 1 cup marinara sauce
- 1 cup ricotta cheese
- 1/2 cup grated mozzarella cheese
- 2 cloves garlic, minced
- 1 tbsp olive oil
- 1/2 tsp dried oregano
- Salt and pepper to taste

Instructions:

1. Preheat oven to 375°F (190°C).
2. Cook pasta according to package instructions; drain and set aside.
3. In a large skillet, heat olive oil over medium heat. Sauté garlic until fragrant, then add fresh spinach until wilted.
4. In a large bowl, combine cooked pasta, spinach, feta cheese, ricotta cheese, marinara sauce, oregano, salt, and pepper.
5. Transfer mixture to a greased baking dish and sprinkle with mozzarella cheese on top.
6. Bake for 25-30 minutes, or until cheese is bubbly and golden.

Coconut Curry Noodles

Ingredients:

- 8 oz rice noodles
- 1 can (14 oz) coconut milk
- 2 tbsp red curry paste
- 1 cup bell peppers, sliced
- 1 cup snap peas
- 1 tbsp soy sauce
- 1 tbsp lime juice
- Fresh basil for garnish
- Sesame seeds for garnish

Instructions:

1. Cook rice noodles according to package instructions; drain and set aside.
2. In a large skillet, combine coconut milk and red curry paste over medium heat. Stir until smooth.
3. Add bell peppers and snap peas; cook for about 5 minutes until vegetables are tender.
4. Stir in soy sauce and lime juice.
5. Add cooked noodles to the skillet; toss to coat evenly.
6. Serve garnished with fresh basil and sesame seeds.

Prawn and Mango Noodle Salad

Ingredients:

- 8 oz rice vermicelli noodles
- 1 lb cooked prawns, peeled and deveined
- 1 ripe mango, diced
- 1 cup cucumber, sliced
- 1/4 cup fresh mint, chopped
- 1/4 cup fresh cilantro, chopped
- 1/4 cup lime juice
- 2 tbsp fish sauce
- 1 tbsp sugar
- 1 tbsp chili sauce (optional)

Instructions:

1. Cook rice vermicelli noodles according to package instructions; drain and rinse under cold water.
2. In a large bowl, combine prawns, diced mango, cucumber, mint, and cilantro.
3. In a separate bowl, whisk together lime juice, fish sauce, sugar, and chili sauce.
4. Add the cooked noodles and dressing to the salad; toss gently to combine.
5. Serve chilled or at room temperature.

Fettuccine Primavera

Ingredients:

- 12 oz fettuccine
- 1 cup bell peppers, sliced
- 1 cup zucchini, sliced
- 1 cup cherry tomatoes, halved
- 1 cup broccoli florets
- 3 cloves garlic, minced
- 1/2 cup grated Parmesan cheese
- 1/4 cup olive oil
- 1/2 tsp Italian seasoning
- Salt and pepper to taste

Instructions:

1. Cook fettuccine according to package instructions; drain and set aside.
2. In a large skillet, heat olive oil over medium heat. Add garlic and sauté until fragrant.
3. Add bell peppers, zucchini, broccoli, and cherry tomatoes; cook until tender (about 5-7 minutes).
4. Add the cooked fettuccine to the skillet; toss to combine with the vegetables.
5. Stir in Parmesan cheese and season with Italian seasoning, salt, and pepper. Serve hot.

Sweet and Spicy Noodles with Peanut Sauce

Ingredients:

- 8 oz egg noodles
- 1/2 cup creamy peanut butter
- 1/4 cup soy sauce
- 2 tbsp honey or maple syrup
- 2 tbsp rice vinegar
- 1 tbsp chili garlic sauce
- 1 cup carrots, shredded
- 1 cup bell peppers, sliced
- 1/4 cup chopped peanuts for garnish

Instructions:

1. Cook egg noodles according to package instructions; drain and set aside.
2. In a small bowl, whisk together peanut butter, soy sauce, honey, rice vinegar, and chili garlic sauce until smooth.
3. In a large bowl, combine cooked noodles, shredded carrots, and bell peppers.
4. Pour peanut sauce over the noodle mixture; toss to coat evenly.
5. Serve garnished with chopped peanuts.

Noodles with Miso Butter and Scallions

Ingredients:

- 8 oz udon or soba noodles
- 3 tbsp unsalted butter
- 2 tbsp white miso paste
- 2 tbsp soy sauce
- 1/4 cup scallions, sliced
- Sesame seeds for garnish

Instructions:

1. Cook noodles according to package instructions; drain and set aside.
2. In a large skillet, melt butter over medium heat. Stir in miso paste and soy sauce until combined.
3. Add cooked noodles to the skillet; toss to coat with miso butter.
4. Remove from heat and stir in sliced scallions.
5. Serve garnished with sesame seeds.

Wild Mushroom and Truffle Oil Pasta

Ingredients:

- 12 oz fettuccine or tagliatelle
- 2 cups mixed wild mushrooms, sliced
- 3 cloves garlic, minced
- 1/2 cup heavy cream
- 1/4 cup grated Parmesan cheese
- 2 tbsp truffle oil
- 2 tbsp olive oil
- Salt and pepper to taste
- Fresh parsley for garnish

Instructions:

1. Cook pasta according to package instructions; drain and set aside.
2. In a large skillet, heat olive oil over medium heat. Sauté garlic until fragrant, then add mushrooms; cook until tender.
3. Stir in heavy cream and bring to a simmer. Add Parmesan cheese, stirring until melted.
4. Add cooked pasta to the skillet; toss to combine and coat with sauce.
5. Drizzle with truffle oil, season with salt and pepper, and garnish with fresh parsley before serving.

Chicken Lo Mein

Ingredients:

- 8 oz lo mein noodles
- 1 lb boneless, skinless chicken breast, sliced
- 1 cup bell peppers, sliced
- 1 cup carrots, julienned
- 1 cup snap peas
- 3 green onions, sliced
- 3 cloves garlic, minced
- 1 tbsp ginger, minced
- 1/4 cup soy sauce
- 2 tbsp oyster sauce
- 1 tbsp sesame oil
- 1 tbsp vegetable oil

Instructions:

1. Cook lo mein noodles according to package instructions; drain and set aside.
2. In a large skillet or wok, heat vegetable oil over medium-high heat. Add sliced chicken and cook until no longer pink.
3. Add garlic and ginger; sauté for 1 minute.
4. Add bell peppers, carrots, and snap peas; stir-fry until vegetables are tender.
5. Add cooked noodles, soy sauce, oyster sauce, and sesame oil; toss to combine and heat through.
6. Serve hot, garnished with green onions.

Sesame Noodles with Grilled Chicken

Ingredients:

- 8 oz spaghetti or udon noodles
- 1 lb grilled chicken breast, sliced
- 1/4 cup sesame oil
- 1/4 cup soy sauce
- 2 tbsp rice vinegar
- 2 tbsp honey
- 1 tbsp chili garlic sauce
- 1 cup cucumber, julienned
- 1/4 cup sesame seeds
- 3 green onions, sliced

Instructions:

1. Cook noodles according to package instructions; drain and set aside.
2. In a bowl, whisk together sesame oil, soy sauce, rice vinegar, honey, and chili garlic sauce.
3. In a large bowl, combine cooked noodles, grilled chicken, cucumber, and the sesame dressing; toss to coat.
4. Serve garnished with sesame seeds and green onions.

Baked Macaroni and Cheese with Bacon

Ingredients:

- 8 oz elbow macaroni
- 4 cups shredded sharp cheddar cheese
- 1/2 cup grated Parmesan cheese
- 4 slices bacon, cooked and crumbled
- 3 cups milk
- 1/4 cup butter
- 1/4 cup all-purpose flour
- 1/2 tsp paprika
- 1/2 tsp salt
- 1/4 tsp black pepper

Instructions:

1. Preheat oven to 350°F (175°C).
2. Cook macaroni according to package instructions; drain and set aside.
3. In a large saucepan, melt butter over medium heat. Whisk in flour and cook for 1-2 minutes.
4. Gradually add milk, whisking constantly until thickened. Stir in cheddar cheese, Parmesan, paprika, salt, and pepper until melted.
5. Combine cooked macaroni and cheese sauce in a baking dish. Top with crumbled bacon.
6. Bake for 20-25 minutes or until bubbly and golden on top.

Lemon Basil Pasta with Grilled Shrimp

Ingredients:

- 8 oz linguine or spaghetti
- 1 lb shrimp, peeled and deveined
- 1/4 cup olive oil
- 2 cloves garlic, minced
- Juice and zest of 1 lemon
- 1/2 cup fresh basil, chopped
- Salt and pepper to taste

Instructions:

1. Cook pasta according to package instructions; drain and set aside.
2. In a bowl, toss shrimp with olive oil, garlic, lemon juice, salt, and pepper.
3. Grill shrimp over medium heat until pink and opaque (about 3-4 minutes per side).
4. In a large bowl, combine cooked pasta, grilled shrimp, lemon zest, and fresh basil; toss to combine.
5. Serve hot, garnished with additional basil if desired.

Spaghetti with Roasted Garlic and Broccoli

Ingredients:

- 12 oz spaghetti
- 1 head of broccoli, cut into florets
- 1 whole head of garlic
- 1/4 cup olive oil
- 1/2 tsp red pepper flakes
- 1/4 cup grated Parmesan cheese
- Salt and pepper to taste

Instructions:

1. Preheat oven to 400°F (200°C).
2. Cut the top off the garlic head, drizzle with olive oil, and wrap in foil. Roast for 30-35 minutes until soft.
3. Cook spaghetti according to package instructions; drain and set aside.
4. Steam broccoli until tender.
5. In a large bowl, squeeze the roasted garlic out of the skins and mash with a fork. Add olive oil, red pepper flakes, salt, and pepper; mix well.
6. Toss spaghetti, roasted garlic mixture, and broccoli together. Serve with grated Parmesan cheese.

Cheesy Italian Pasta Bake

Ingredients:

- 12 oz penne pasta
- 2 cups marinara sauce
- 2 cups shredded mozzarella cheese
- 1 cup ricotta cheese
- 1/2 cup grated Parmesan cheese
- 1/2 lb Italian sausage, cooked and crumbled
- 1 tsp Italian seasoning
- Fresh basil for garnish

Instructions:

1. Preheat oven to 375°F (190°C).
2. Cook penne pasta according to package instructions; drain and set aside.
3. In a large bowl, combine cooked pasta, marinara sauce, Italian sausage, ricotta cheese, Italian seasoning, and half of the mozzarella cheese.
4. Transfer the mixture to a greased baking dish and top with remaining mozzarella and Parmesan cheese.
5. Bake for 25-30 minutes or until cheese is bubbly and golden.
6. Garnish with fresh basil before serving.

Vegetable Lo Mein

Ingredients:

- 8 oz lo mein noodles
- 1 cup bell peppers, sliced
- 1 cup carrots, julienned
- 1 cup broccoli florets
- 1 cup bean sprouts
- 3 cloves garlic, minced
- 1 tbsp ginger, minced
- 1/4 cup soy sauce
- 2 tbsp sesame oil
- 1 tbsp vegetable oil

Instructions:

1. Cook lo mein noodles according to package instructions; drain and set aside.
2. In a large skillet or wok, heat vegetable oil over medium-high heat. Add garlic and ginger; sauté for 1 minute.
3. Add bell peppers, carrots, and broccoli; stir-fry until tender.
4. Add bean sprouts, cooked noodles, soy sauce, and sesame oil; toss to combine and heat through.
5. Serve hot.

Alfredo Zoodles (Zucchini Noodles)

Ingredients:

- 4 medium zucchinis, spiralized
- 1 cup heavy cream
- 1/2 cup grated Parmesan cheese
- 2 cloves garlic, minced
- 2 tbsp butter
- Salt and pepper to taste
- Fresh parsley for garnish

Instructions:

1. In a large skillet, melt butter over medium heat. Add garlic and sauté until fragrant.
2. Pour in heavy cream and bring to a simmer; stir in Parmesan cheese until melted and smooth.
3. Add spiralized zucchini noodles to the skillet; cook for 2-3 minutes until just tender.
4. Season with salt and pepper.
5. Serve hot, garnished with fresh parsley.

Pasta with Roasted Red Pepper Sauce

Ingredients:

- 12 oz pasta (spaghetti or penne)
- 2 large red bell peppers, roasted (jarred or homemade)
- 1/2 cup heavy cream or coconut cream
- 2 tbsp olive oil
- 3 cloves garlic, minced
- 1/4 cup grated Parmesan cheese (optional)
- Salt and pepper to taste
- Fresh basil or parsley for garnish

Instructions:

1. **Cook the Pasta:**
   - Cook the pasta according to package instructions; drain and set aside.
2. **Prepare the Sauce:**
   - In a blender, combine the roasted red peppers, heavy cream, olive oil, garlic, salt, and pepper. Blend until smooth.
   - If using, stir in grated Parmesan cheese for extra creaminess.
3. **Heat the Sauce:**
   - In a skillet over medium heat, pour the roasted red pepper sauce. Bring it to a gentle simmer, stirring occasionally.
4. **Combine:**
   - Add the cooked pasta to the sauce, tossing until the pasta is well coated.
5. **Serve:**
   - Garnish with fresh basil or parsley. Serve hot.

Black Bean Noodles with Avocado and Lime

Ingredients:

- 8 oz black bean noodles (or other gluten-free noodles)
- 1 ripe avocado, diced
- Juice of 2 limes
- 1 cup cherry tomatoes, halved
- 1/2 cup corn (canned or frozen)
- 1/4 cup fresh cilantro, chopped
- 1 tbsp olive oil
- Salt and pepper to taste

Instructions:

1. **Cook the Noodles:**
    - Cook the black bean noodles according to package instructions; drain and rinse under cold water to cool.
2. **Prepare the Dressing:**
    - In a small bowl, whisk together lime juice, olive oil, salt, and pepper.
3. **Combine Ingredients:**
    - In a large bowl, combine the cooked noodles, diced avocado, cherry tomatoes, corn, and cilantro.
4. **Dress the Salad:**
    - Pour the lime dressing over the noodle mixture and toss gently to combine.
5. **Serve:**
    - Serve immediately, garnished with additional cilantro if desired.